7 TRANSFORMATIONAL LESSONS FOR PERSONAL GROWTH

GANDHI'S GUIDE

DEDICATION

To the champions of peace and non-violence movements.
This book stands as a tribute to your unwavering commitment, echoing
Gandhi's wisdom, and shedding light on paths of understanding, resilience,
and unity. With heartfelt gratitude, it's dedicated to your tireless endeavors in
shaping a tomorrow rooted in compassion, courage, and steadfastness.

CONTENTS

INTRODUCTION

"Cultivation of minds should be the ultimate aim of human existence." - Mahatma Gandhi

Mahatma Gandhi, born in 1869, stands as an iconic figure whose influence extends far beyond the borders of his home country, India. He emerged as a pivotal figure during India's fervent struggle against colonial rule, shaping the trajectory of the nation's journey toward independence. His unyielding commitment to principles such as nonviolence, truth, and simplicity didn't merely echo within the Indian subcontinent but resonated profoundly across the globe.

Gandhi's unwavering faith in nonviolence wasn't just a philosophy; it was a deeply ingrained belief that served as the cornerstone of his fight against oppression. His advocacy for nonviolent resistance, famously known as Satyagraha, advocated peaceful protests and civil disobedience as potent instruments for social and political change. This radical yet profoundly humane approach not only transformed India's struggle for independence but also left an enduring legacy that inspired countless movements for freedom and justice worldwide.

The essence of truth and its intrinsic link to Gandhi's philosophy reverberated in his famous quote, "Truth is

God." He regarded truth not merely as an abstract concept but as an inherent principle that guides and shapes one's actions and beliefs. His unwavering commitment to truthfulness, both in personal conduct and societal reform, set an exemplary standard for ethical and moral living.

Simplicity was another hallmark of Gandhi's life. He chose to live a modest, austere lifestyle, embodying the very ideals he preached. For him, simplicity was not a lack of possessions but a deliberate choice to detach from materialism and embrace a life focused on essential values and principles.

Gandhi's influence transcended political boundaries: it

became a beacon of hope and inspiration for countless individuals striving for personal growth, societal change, and spiritual enlightenment. His teachings laid the groundwork for a transformative approach to life, emphasizing the innate power within everyone to effectuate change through unwavering commitment to one's beliefs and values.

In the realm of personal growth, Gandhi's emphasis on nonviolence, truth, and simplicity becomes an allegory for adaptability. Just as Gandhi adopted nonviolent methods to challenge the status quo and achieve freedom, individuals can adapt their approaches to life's challenges, fostering resilience, personal evolution, and profound growth.

This thought-provoking book encompasses an astonishing compilation of not just one, but seven awe-inspiring transformational lessons, all of which are firmly rooted in Gandhi's resolute commitment to nonviolence, simplicity, truth, and selfless service. These exceptionally enlightening lessons are masterfully crafted to serve as an indispensable compass, expertly guiding and directing readers towards leading an incredibly purposeful, deeply gratifying, and truly meaningful life that surpasses all expectations.

LESSON ONE:
THE POWER OF NONVIOLENCE

"Nonviolence is the greatest force at the disposal of mankind. It is mightier than the mightiest weapon of destruction devised by the ingenuity of man."

- Mahatma Gandhi.

Exploring Ahimsa: A Way of Being

Ahimsa, Gandhi's profound gift to humanity, encapsulates the priceless principle of nonviolence. More than a mere philosophy, it stands as a transformative way of life with boundless potential to revolutionize our existence.

Ahimsa, also known as nonviolence, extends far beyond

abstaining from physical harm; it embodies a

comprehensive principle that encompasses thoughts,

actions, and words. This guiding principle reflects an

unwavering commitment to compassion, understanding,

and empathy, fostering a profound influence on both

individuals and the global community.

Gandhi's vision of ahimsa isn't just a concept; it's a potent

force that, when embraced, has the remarkable ability to

shape individuals and ripple through the very fabric of

humanity. Ahimsa represents a profound commitment to

compassion, understanding, and empathy. It signifies the

recognition that in our interdependent global community,

every individual action reverberates through the very fabric of humanity.

Gandhi was a humble, seemingly insignificant individual who fearlessly defied an empire, not through force, but through the indomitable might of nonviolence. His remarkable existence epitomized the profound influence that opting for peace instead of hostility can wield.

Practical Applications in Daily Life

Now, let's embrace this philosophy in our daily lives, in every little aspect. Nonviolence is not just for big moments; it flourishes in the small details of our interactions. Let's think about the influence of our words and actions in our workplace, home, and community.

How can we embody ahimsa in the way we communicate, handle conflicts, and nurture relationships?

Picture a regular day: a heated exchange with a colleague, an annoying traffic encounter, or a disagreement at home.

Now, envision the incredible difference it would make if you embraced nonviolence in these moments.

How would your reactions change if you consciously approached each situation with unwavering understanding and boundless compassion?

Interactive Exercises: Reflecting and Applying Nonviolent Principles

Now, let's roll up our sleeves and get practical. Grab a journal or open a new document on your device. Think back to a recent conflict or challenging situation in your life. It could be a disagreement with a friend, a family member, or a colleague.

1. Reflect: Describe the situation in detail.

How did it make you feel?

What were the triggers for conflict?

Be honest with yourself.

2. Identify Nonviolent Alternatives: Now, reimagine the

scenario.

How could nonviolence have played a role?

What words or actions could you have chosen to foster understanding instead of discord?

3. Set an Intention: Choose one nonviolent principle you'd like to incorporate into your interactions moving forward.

It could be active listening, expressing empathy, or seeking common ground.

LESSON TWO: LIVING A SIMPLE LIFE

"Earth provides enough to satisfy every man's need, but not every man's greed." - Mahatma Gandhi.

Gandhi's Emphasis on Simplicity

In a world intricately woven with complexity and diversity, this book extends a heartfelt invitation to embrace the captivating allure of simplicity. It beckons us onto an extraordinary journey, offering a pathway that leads not only to a simpler life but to a profound understanding of its inherent richness.

Consider a life not measured by the abundance of possessions but by the richness found in cherished moments, meaningful connections, and a sense of inner peace. Amid a world clamoring for attention, simplicity invites us to discern between what's essential and what's fleeting. It's a call to strip away the layers of superfluous distractions, revealing the innate beauty hidden beneath the noise of modernity.

Embracing simplicity isn't about renouncing modern comforts; it's about embracing a mindset that transcends materialism. It's a conscious choice to seek fulfillment in experiences rather than acquisitions, in moments of stillness rather than in constant motion. Simplicity becomes a beacon guiding us toward a life not burdened by excess but enriched by purpose, contentment, and a profound sense of clarity.

Gandhi, adorned in his humble attire amidst a world of opulence, stands as an emblem of simplicity's transformative power. His life serves as a testament to the immense fulfillment derived from embracing life's essentials. Yet, simplicity for Gandhi wasn't merely about shunning material excess; it was an invigorating mindset— a conscious choice to unshackle oneself from the burdens of a cluttered existence.

It's an endeavor to create space—not just physical but mental and emotional—a canvas on which the colors of life's true essence can vividly shine. In this pursuit, simplicity becomes a conduit to deeper self-awareness, fostering a genuine connection with oneself and the world around us.

Practical Tips for simplifying life.

Let's explore together practical methods for simplifying different aspects of our lives. From organizing physical spaces to optimizing daily routines, simplicity can take shape in countless ways. Take a moment to think about your daily routine - have you ever considered how simplifying it could bring you more peace and clarity?

Interactive exercise: crafting your personal simplicity plan.

Now, let's roll up our sleeves and start crafting your simplicity plan. Grab a notebook or open a new document.

1. Inventory: Take stock of your living space, your possessions, and your daily schedule. What items or activities bring true value and joy to your life?

2. Declutter: Identify areas where you can declutter - whether it's your closet, your digital space, or your commitments. What can you let go of to create more space for what truly matters?

3. Prioritize: Choose three key areas where you want to

embrace simplicity. It could be your physical space, your daily habits, or your commitments.

4. Action Steps: Break down these areas into actionable steps. For instance, if it's decluttering your living space, schedule specific times for sorting through belongings.

5. Reflection: Regularly reflect on your progress. How does simplifying these areas impact your life? What joys and newfound perspectives emerge?

Simplicity isn't merely about deprivation or lack; it encompasses an immense abundance - an abundance of spaciousness, ample time, and profound clarity. As you embark on this transformative journey towards embracing a simpler life, let us not forget the timeless example set by

Gandhi. Embrace simplicity not as a mere restriction, but

rather as a magnificent gateway that leads to an even more

enriching and profoundly fulfilling existence.

LESSON THREE:
THE UNIVERSALITY OF TRUTH

"Truth stands, even if there be no public support. It is self-sustained."
- Mahatma Gandhi.

Understanding satyagraha: the force of truth.

Satyagraha, an enlightening concept often attributed to the revered Mahatma Gandhi, passionately underscores the universality of truth. In Lesson three, we meticulously explore the profound influence of Satyagraha and its undeniable connection to personal development, fervently

drawing inspiration from the timeless teachings of

Mahatma Gandhi. We embark on a captivating

journey to discover the awe-inspiring

transformative power of truth. With utmost

finesse, we endeavor to craft a compelling narrative

that revolves around authenticity and unwavering

moral integrity.

Satyagraha is an awe-inspiring concept that

transcends mere rejection of falsehood. It

embodies an unwavering power and resolute

commitment to truth in every sphere of our lives.

It wholeheartedly embraces the profound belief

that truth possesses an extraordinary capacity to

enlighten and liberate us, both individually and as a

global community. Let us recognize and embrace

the transformative potential of Satyagraha, as it

holds the key to unlocking a brighter, more

enlightened world for all.

Exploring personal honesty and authenticity.

Let's explore this idea on a personal level. How often do we find ourselves wearing masks, portraying versions of ourselves that deviate from who we truly are? Authentic living encourages us to peel off these layers and wholeheartedly embrace our genuine selves. Take a moment to reflect on instances when you may have hesitated to express your truth, either in conversations or within your own mind. What were the fears or insecurities that led you to hold back?

Interactive exercise: reflecting on personal truths.

Now, let's embark on an introspective journey. Take out your journal or create a dedicated space for reflection.

1. Self-Reflection: Write about a situation where you might have compromised your truth. How did it make you feel? What fears or pressures influenced your actions?

2. Authenticity Check: Assess different aspects of your life - work, relationships, personal beliefs. Are

there areas where you're not living in alignment with your truth?

3. Commitment to Truth: Set an intention to embrace truthfulness in one aspect of your life. It could be expressing your opinions honestly or being more transparent in relationships.

Remember, the pursuit of truth is a process, not an endpoint. As you navigate this journey of authenticity and honesty, channel Gandhi's unwavering commitment to truth as a guiding light toward a more fulfilling and genuine existence.

LESSON FOUR:
SELF-DISCIPLINE AND SELF-CONTROL

Strength does not come from physical capacity. It comes from an indomitable will." - Mahatma Gandi

Gandhi's teaching on self-discipline and self-control.

L et us dive into the profound teachings of self-discipline and self-control as exemplified by Mahatma Gandhi is an enlightening journey that traverses the realm of personal development. Gandhi's life stands as an epitome of inner strength and deliberate control over one's actions and thoughts, offering us invaluable lessons on the power of self-discipline.

Gandhi's teachings on self-discipline transcend the conventional understanding of restraint. They encapsulate a conscious and deliberate choice to govern every aspect of one's being—mind, actions, and emotions. It wasn't merely about adhering to a routine; it was a resolute commitment to aligning one's conduct with deeply held principles and values.

In envisioning Gandhi's dedication to his beliefs, his unwavering commitment to truth and justice becomes apparent. His ability to withstand adversity, persevere in the face of challenges, and stay true to his convictions were manifestations of profound self-discipline and self-control.

Even amid the most trying circumstances, Gandhi's inner strength remained unshaken, a testament to the power of disciplined thoughts and actions.

His life wasn't devoid of temptations or trials; rather, it was a conscious choice to navigate these challenges with unwavering resolve and an indomitable will. His disciplined approach wasn't restrictive but empowering, granting him the strength to stay aligned with his principles even in the face of opposition.

Picture Gandhi's journey—a deliberate and disciplined march toward truth and justice. His disciplined mindset wasn't a rigid structure but a flexible framework that allowed for adaptability without compromising his core values. This adaptability, rooted in self-discipline, enabled him to navigate complexities while staying true to his principles.

Gandhi's teachings on self-discipline transcend generations, offering timeless wisdom for personal growth and inner resilience. They remind us that true strength doesn't solely emanate from physical prowess but springs from the unwavering commitment to exercise self-control over our thoughts, actions, and emotions. It's this inner fortitude that propels us toward self-discovery, empowerment, and a life guided by conscious choices.

As we immerse ourselves in Lesson Four, let Gandhi's profound teachings on self-discipline and self-control serve as guiding beacons illuminating the path toward genuine growth, resilience, and the unleashing of our authentic capabilities. Let us harness the transformative power of self-discipline, sculpting our lives with intention, purpose, and unwavering determination.

Strategies for developing self-discipline.

Hey there! Let's explore some super practical strategies that can totally help us become more self-disciplined. We'll chat about creating awesome habits and setting boundaries that really empower us to tap into our inner strength. Sound good? Let's get started! Let's think about those parts of your

life where self-discipline can be a bit tough. How can we

turn these challenges into exciting chances for personal

growth?

Mindfulness exercises for building self-control

 Mindfulness can truly be our trusted companion when it

comes to mastering self-control. By nurturing a gentle

awareness of our thoughts and impulses, we empower

ourselves to consciously respond rather than hastily react.

Let's embrace this wonderful tool for a more mindful

approach to life!

Picture a moment of temptation - a situation where self-control wavers. But what if, in that very moment, you could simply take a pause, calmly observe the impulse, and consciously make a choice that aligns perfectly with your values?

Interactive exercise: Creating your self-discipline plan.

Now, let's craft your personal self-discipline plan. Grab your journal or create a dedicated space for reflection.

1. Self-Assessment: Identify areas where self-discipline is lacking or needed. It could be related to health, work, relationships, or personal growth.

2. Define Goals: Set clear, achievable goals that align with

your values. Break them down into smaller, actionable steps.

3. Habit Formation: Cultivate positive habits that support your goals. Start small and gradually build on them.

4. Mindfulness Practice: Incorporate mindfulness exercises into your routine. Practice being present and observing your impulses without judgment.

5. Reflection and Adaptation: Regularly review your progress. Celebrate successes and learn from challenges. Adjust your plan as needed.

Remember, self-discipline is a muscle that strengthens with practice. As you embark on this journey of cultivating self-discipline, let this steadfast resolve guide you towards a life

guided by conscious choices and inner strength.

LESSON FIVE: EMBRACING HUMILITY

"True humility means most strenuous and constant endeavor entirely directed towards the service of humanity, without the slightest desire for self-aggrandizement."
- Mahatma Gandhi

Humility and Service-Oriented Mindset.

Gandhi, a beacon of humility and service, stood as an exemplar of selflessness amidst the tumultuous tides of history. His legacy reverberates through time, not merely for his political prowess or ideological fervor but for the profound humility that underpinned his every action. The cornerstone of Gandhi's life was his unwavering commitment to service, a commitment steeped in humility that transformed him into a towering figure of inspiration.

In exploring Gandhi's humility, one encounters a humility rooted not in self-effacement but in a profound understanding of interconnectedness. Gandhi recognized that true greatness lay not in the pursuit of power or acclaim but in service to others. He embodied this ethos, shunning opulence and embracing simplicity, demonstrating that humility was not a mark of weakness but a source of strength. His austere lifestyle, characterized by simple attire and a spartan existence, spoke volumes about his commitment to a life devoid of material excess.

Central to Gandhi's humility was his unwavering belief in the power of empathy and compassion. He walked alongside the downtrodden, identifying with their struggles and championing their cause. His famous words, "The best way to find yourself is to lose yourself in the service of others," encapsulate his philosophy, emphasizing that true fulfillment lay in selflessly serving humanity.

Moreover, Gandhi's humility was a catalyst for his visionary leadership. He didn't seek authority for personal gain but to amplify the voices of the marginalized. His leadership was inclusive, inviting participation from all strata of society. His humility wasn't a mere façade but a genuine ethos that resonated in his interactions, fostering trust and unity among diverse groups.

Gandhi's humility wasn't passive; it was an active force driving his commitment to service. He believed that genuine transformation arises from the collective elevation of society, achieved through relentless service. His initiatives, such as the salt march and his commitment to nonviolent resistance, were embodiments of this principle—a testament to his belief that even in the face of oppression, humility and service could be potent tools for change. Furthermore, Gandhi's humility reverberated beyond his immediate actions; it permeated the very fabric of his movement. He inspired countless individuals to embrace humility and service, fostering a legacy that transcends time and continues to inspire generations to prioritize the well-being of others over personal gain.

In essence, Gandhi's humility was not a passive trait but an active force that fueled his unwavering commitment to service. It was the bedrock upon which his transformative journey rested, illuminating the path towards a more compassionate, equitable world.

As we embark on our own journeys, embracing the lessons that Gandhi's humility and service-oriented mindset offer us, let us recognize that true greatness lies not in the spotlight but in the shadows where one quietly serves others.

The Importance of Humility in Personal Growth.

Being humble isn't a weakness at all; it's a true indicator of strength. It helps us stay self-aware and encourages us to always be open to learning and growing. Embracing humility allows us to welcome new perspectives and experiences with open arms. Let's think about those times when embracing humility helped us grow as individuals. How did being humble open doors to fresh insights or exciting opportunities? Share your experiences!

Practicing Humility in Daily Interactions.

Hey, how about we embrace humility in our everyday lives? It's in those little, seemingly unimportant moments where humility truly stands out in how we treat others, how we respond, and how open we are to learning from everyone we meet.

Group Activity: Sharing Stories of Humility and Service.

Let's come together for a wonderful journey of humility and service. Join your loved ones, friends, or colleagues and let's share heartwarming stories or personal experiences where humility made a remarkable difference. It's time to create meaningful connections and embrace the power of humility together! Imagine a beautiful gathering where everyone shares heartfelt stories about how humility has brought people closer and brought about incredible transformations. How might these shared experiences inspire and strengthen our understanding of one another? Embrace the transformative power of humility, as it ignites personal growth and cultivates deep connections with the world. Let humility be your driving force, propelling you towards a life of service and leaving a lasting impact.

LESSON SIX:
RESILIENCE IN THE FACE OF ADVERSITY

"The difference between what we do and what we are capable of doing would suffice to solve most of the world's problems."
- Mahatma Gandhi

Strategies for Building Resilience.

This chapter brings us face to face with one of the most remarkable qualities embodied by Gandhi: resilience. His life was the epitome of unwavering determination in the face of seemingly insurmountable obstacles. Gandhi didn't merely weather the storms; he thrived in adversity, demonstrating that resilience isn't just about endurance but about harnessing strength and growth from every trial.

Gandhi's resilience was forged through the fires of countless challenges. Whether it was leading a nation to independence against the mighty British Empire or enduring imprisonment and personal hardships, his resolve remained unshaken. His resilience wasn't passive; it was an active force that fueled his unwavering commitment to his principles.

Understanding and emulating Gandhi's resilience requires a grasp of practical strategies that fortify this attribute within us. One such strategy is fostering a growth mindset—a belief that challenges are opportunities for growth rather than insurmountable barriers. Gandhi epitomized this by viewing obstacles as chances for personal and societal evolution. Cultivating a similar mindset enables us to reframe setbacks as steppingstones toward resilience.

Moreover, building robust support networks is another cornerstone of resilience. Gandhi drew strength from the collective efforts of a dedicated team and the unwavering support of his followers. Similarly, surrounding oneself with supportive friends, family, or communities can provide the necessary encouragement and perspective during trying times, enhancing our ability to bounce back from adversity.

Reflecting on personal experiences can illuminate the transformative potential of embracing resilience. Consider a recent challenge you encountered. What if, instead of succumbing to despair, you approached it with Gandhi's resilient spirit? How might your outlook have shifted? Would you have perceived the challenge as an opportunity for growth rather than an insurmountable hurdle? Imagining this scenario underscores the transformative impact a resilient mindset could have had on the entire experience. Embracing resilience doesn't entail denying the gravity of challenges or suppressing emotions; rather, it involves acknowledging difficulties while actively seeking ways to navigate them. Gandhi himself experienced moments of despair but never allowed them to overshadow his commitment to his principles. His resilience stemmed from an unwavering belief in the righteousness of his cause and an unyielding spirit that refused to be subdued by adversity.

Furthermore, Gandhi's resilience was deeply intertwined with his ability to adapt. He recognized that rigid adherence to a singular approach could be futile in the face of ever-changing circumstances. His flexibility allowed him to pivot strategies without compromising his principles—a testament to the adaptive nature of resilience.

Gandhi's life serves as a testament to the transformative power of resilience. By fostering a growth mindset, cultivating strong support networks, and envisioning challenges as opportunities for growth, we can embrace resilience as a guiding force in navigating life's adversities.

As we tread our own paths, let us draw inspiration from Gandhi's indomitable spirit, recognizing that resilience isn't merely about enduring hardships but about emerging stronger and more steadfast from them.

Are there real-life stories of resilience that you could relate to? where individuals gracefully and determinedly overcame adversity. These stories could inspire and guide us through our own challenges, shining as beacons of inspiration. How do you think these narratives would connect with your own personal journey?

Interactive Exercise: Setting Resilient Goals

Now, let's kickstart an exciting goal-setting exercise focused on building resilience! Make sure you grab your favorite journal or create a cozy space dedicated to reflection.

1. Self-Assessment: Identify areas in your life where increased resilience is needed. Is it in your career, relationships, health, or personal development?

2. Resilient Goals: Define resilient goals - objectives that

challenge you while fostering strength and growth. Break them down into smaller, actionable steps.

3. Mindset Shift: Adopt a growth mindset - see challenges as opportunities for learning and growth rather than setbacks.

4. Support System: Build a support network surround yourself with individuals who uplift and encourage resilience.

5. Reflection and Adaptation: Regularly assess your progress. Celebrate resilience in action and adjust goals as needed.

Resilience is not just about getting through tough times; it's about flourishing even in the face of adversity. As you begin

this path towards becoming more resilient, let Gandhi's

unwavering determination be a source of inspiration to turn

challenges into opportunities for personal growth and

happiness.

LESSON SEVEN:
COMPASSION AND SERVICE

"Service which is rendered without joy helps neither the servant nor the served. But all other pleasures and possessions pale into nothingness before service which is rendered in a spirit of joy." - Mahatma Gandhi.

Commitment to Service and Compassion.

Hey there! Prepare yourself to unlock the doors to an exquisitely fulfilling life as we embark on a captivating exploration of the profound secrets of compassion and service. Brace yourself for an awe-inspiring journey as we delve into the extraordinary transformative power of selfless acts.

Gandhi's commitment to service and compassion was the cornerstone of his extraordinary life. His unwavering dedication to alleviating the plight of others, regardless of their circumstances, epitomized the essence of humanity itself. Envision Gandhi walking among the marginalized, his every step resonating with an unyielding commitment to relieve suffering and uplift the downtrodden. His boundless compassion wasn't just a virtue; it was a guiding principle that shaped his every decision and action.

Central to Gandhi's ethos was the belief that true fulfillment and purpose lie in service to others. His life was a testament to this belief, as he tirelessly worked towards social justice, championing the cause of the oppressed and marginalized.

His famous Salt March and advocacy for nonviolent resistance were demonstrations of his commitment to service—a service that wasn't bound by boundaries or limitations but transcended societal barriers.

Gandhi's compassion extended beyond mere empathy; it was an active force that spurred action. His life was a living embodiment of the philosophy that in serving others, one finds the true essence of one's humanity. His compassion wasn't reserved for the select few but encompassed all, irrespective of caste, creed, or social status.

Furthermore, Gandhi's commitment to service and

compassion ignited a ripple effect, inspiring countless others to follow suit. His actions served as a beacon, illuminating the path for individuals to embrace empathy and kindness. His leadership wasn't authoritarian but rooted in humility and service, encouraging others to step forward and make a difference in their communities.

The transformative power of Gandhi's approach to compassion and service lies not only in the impact on society but also in the profound personal fulfillment it brings. Imagine the joy and contentment Gandhi felt, knowing that his life was dedicated to serving a higher purpose, to being a catalyst for positive change in the world.

Picture Gandhi strolling amidst the marginalized, his unwavering commitment to relieving suffering radiating through his every move! His boundless compassion served as a guiding light, inspiring others to embrace empathy and spread kindness.

Incorporating Service into Daily Life.

Service goes beyond grand gestures; it thrives through the small acts that are intricately woven into our daily routines. From simply lending a listening ear to generously volunteering our time, there are countless ways to fill our lives with compassion. Let's think about how we can sprinkle moments of service throughout our day. How could a small act of kindness bring a little sunshine to someone else's day?

Acts of Kindness Challenge.

Join us in an exhilarating acts of kindness challenge - an extraordinary journey that uplifts the soul through selfless gestures. It is within these seemingly small acts that the immense waves of compassion ripple out, profoundly impacting lives and fostering a profound sense of interconnectedness. Imagine yourself doing a simple act of kindness every day. Just think about how these actions can create a beautiful ripple effect, inspiring others to spread compassion and make the world a better place!

Interactive Exercise: Creating a Personal Compassion

Plan.

Now, let's craft your personal compassion plan. Grab your journal or create a dedicated space for reflection.

1. Reflect on Values: Identify causes or values that resonate with you. What aspects of service and compassion align with your beliefs?

2. Identify Opportunities: Look for opportunities in your community or surroundings where you can contribute. It could be volunteering, supporting a cause, or aiding someone in need.

3. Set Goals: Define tangible, achievable goals for

incorporating service and compassion into your life. Start

with small, manageable steps.

4. Regular Practice: Make compassion a habit. Engage in

acts of service regularly, integrating them into your routine.

5. Reflection and Impact: Reflect on the impact of your

actions. How does service and compassion enrich your life

and the lives of others? As you embark on this journey of

compassion and service, let Gandhi's dedication to selfless

acts guide you toward a life enriched by empathy, kindness,

and a deep sense of purpose.

CONCLUSION

Wow! Congratulations on successfully completing this incredible personal development guide! By embracing the seven transformative lessons inspired by the remarkable life and teachings of Mahatma Gandhi, you have embarked on an exhilarating journey towards self-discovery, boundless growth, and a truly fulfilling existence!

Mahatma Gandhi's legacy is not just a piece of history; it's a beautiful reminder of the timeless strength of human values. From the unwavering power of nonviolence to the simple joy of living, and from the honesty of truthfulness to the strength in facing challenges, his teachings touch the hearts of people from every generation. They offer invaluable wisdom, guiding us towards a truly meaningful and happy life.

As you progressed through each lesson, you explored the practical applications of Gandhi's principles in your daily life. The concept of nonviolence, the value of simplicity, the importance of truthfulness, the inner strength derived from self-discipline, the fostering of connections through humility, the ability to persevere in difficult times, and the unifying power of compassion—all these aspects have initiated a transformative process within you.

Thank you so much for joining us on this incredible journey inspired by Mahatma Gandhi! As you continue this path, may you embrace the essence of these lessons, creating a life brimming with purpose, fulfillment, and a wholehearted dedication to making positive changes. Cheers to an amazing adventure ahead.

ABOUT THE AUTHOR

The Author wears multiple hats: a devoted husband and a loving father of two amazing boys. He's a doctor, preacher, mentor, and life guide. Within the pages of this book, he effortlessly intertwines Gandhi's timeless wisdom with his extensive experience in healing, teaching, and guiding.

Embodying Gandhi's principles in both personal and professional realms, the Author presents more than just lessons; his book is a profound roadmap to self-realization and empowerment.

Printed in Great Britain
by Amazon

33707707R00044